W9-AQZ-837

Hickory Flat Public Library
2740 East Cherokee Drive
Canton, GA 30115

Everything You Need to Know About Eating Smart

Adopting a healthy diet can improve your life in many ways.

Everything You Need to Know About Eating Smart

Aileen Weintraub

Rosen Publishing Group, Inc./New York

To Natasha, Andrea, Melissa, Ed, George, and Kirk, my Muses.

Published in 2000 by The Rosen Publishing Group, Inc.
29 East 21st Street, New York, NY 10010

Copyright © 2000 by The Rosen Publishing Group, Inc.

First Edition

Library of Congress Cataloging-in-Publication Data

Weintraub, Aileen, 1973–
    Everything you need to know about eating smart / Aileen Weintraub.
        p.   cm. — (The need to know library)
    Includes bibliographical references and index.
    Summary: Discusses dietary and nutritional health, healthy eating habits, food pyramids, and ways to stay healthy.
    ISBN 0-8239-3082-3 (lib. bdg.)
    1. Nutrition—Juvenile literature.   2. Health—Nutritional aspects—Juvenile literature.   3. Food—Juvenile literature.   [1. Nutrition. 2. Health. 3. Food.]   I. Title. II. Title: Eating Smart.   III. Series.
RA784.W443 200
613.2—dc21   99-16802
                                                                                    CIP

Manufactured in the United States of America

Contents

Introduction

It is hard to worry about eating right when you are a teenager; so many other things seem more important. However, it is essential to have a healthy balance in your life. This can easily be accomplished by becoming more aware of what you eat and your food choices. The foods you eat affect your bones, your muscles, and even your complexion. The sooner you learn about eating the right foods, the sooner you will increase your chances of having a longer, healthier life. Don't worry—learning how to eat smart will not cut into your time to deal with other important matters. You will still have plenty of time and energy for school, your friends, your crush, and your part-time job. In fact, when you eat smart, you have more energy than ever!

For starters, you should know that there are five

basic food groups, each serving an important purpose. When combined, these groups give you all the essential vitamins and minerals that you need.

Eating right is good for both the body and the mind. Your teenage years are busy ones. You need to be focused and alert each and every day. Did you know that too much caffeine can make you feel jumpy and irritable? Or that when you abuse alcohol, you are not only damaging internal organs like your liver but also your sense of clarity? It's easy to fall into the habit of eating fast food, especially since most fast food is relatively inexpensive and involves no preparation. In the long run, however, this type of food does not provide you with good nourishment.

People choose to eat certain foods for many reasons, including taste preference, habit, a particular social situation, or nutritional value. Having enough money for food is another issue for teenagers. It is a lot easier to grab a cheeseburger after school with your friends than it is to make a trip to the supermarket and pick up the ingredients for a healthy meal. This book will show you that there are many options and creative alternatives to choose from when you are trying to eat smart.

Often people use food as a substitute for things other than nourishment. Food plays a large part in celebrations and socializing. Because it is so frequently associated with comfort, many people turn to food for consolation during times of stress or unhappiness.

Too much caffeine can make you edgy, nervous, and irritable.

People also tend to eat when they are bored. Eating when you are not hungry is an unhealthy habit. It is important to recognize why you are eating. If you find that you frequently eat even though you are not hungry, it is time to change that habit. This book can help you do so.

Eating well is a lifestyle choice. Learning how to eat smart *now,* while you are young, will have a positive effect on your future. Once you change your bad habits, you will feel better both mentally and physically, have more energy, decrease your risk for certain illnesses and diseases, and live a healthier life.

Occasional treats have their place in a well-rounded diet.

Chapter One

The Mind-Body Connection

What you put in your body determines how you will look and feel. When you eat a balanced diet, it shows: You have more energy, your skin has a natural glow, your hair looks healthier, and overall you feel good about yourself. Of course, this doesn't mean that you have to ban tasty treats from your diet. After all, who can resist an ice cream sundae with double-chocolate fudge and extra whipped cream every once in a while?

The key to a healthy lifestyle is moderation. This means that it's perfectly okay to have greasy french fries on occasion. However, eating them every day can make you feel sluggish, raise your cholesterol (a buildup of fat in the arteries), and eventually cause you to gain weight. Remember that the food you eat today will affect how you feel tomorrow. As you grow, your body continuously forms bones, muscles, and skin. What you eat determines how all of these things develop.

An important part of eating is enjoying what you eat. Food should taste good and should also satisfy your appetite. If you eat something simply because you think that it is good for you, you will probably not feel satisfied. It's fun to experiment with new foods, but if you know that you hate bananas, don't buy them! They will only end up rotting in your kitchen. Eating smart is about making smart choices.

There are many things to know about the foods you eat. Different foods provide different sources of nutrition. If you eat tuna fish every day, you may be getting enough protein—but what about all those other important things your body needs, like carbohydrates, fiber, and essential vitamins and minerals? Eating a balanced diet will provide you with all of the nutrients you need.

Why Food Affects the Way You Feel

Gail stayed up all night studying for her English test. The next morning, she skipped breakfast so that she would have time to review her notes before class. During the exam, Gail was so tired that she could barely concentrate, and her stomach was growling loudly. When the exam was over, she went straight to the vending machine and grabbed

Fatty, sugary foods can cause your energy level to crash.

a soda and a chocolate bar. By lunchtime she wasn't hungry, but she had no energy at all; the snack didn't seem to have helped. For the rest of the afternoon, Gail could hardly keep her eyes open. When her French teacher called on her, she couldn't even answer an easy question about a verb tense. After school, Gail's friends wanted to go to the mall, but Gail was feeling too cranky.

"All I want to do is go home and sleep," she told her friends.

The food you eat affects how you will feel throughout the day. If you skip breakfast, you might feel yourself struggling to stay awake by 10:30 AM. If you have a can of soda and a chocolate bar for lunch (like Gail did), you will probably end up with what is known as a sugar high: You feel a burst of energy because the sugar is running through your bloodstream. Unfortunately sugar highs don't last very long. Once they are over, you will feel tired and sluggish. The same is true when you go a whole day without food. You will find yourself unable to concentrate; you may be clumsy, feel irritable, or experience hunger pangs. This is because the fasting has caused your blood sugar to drop, forcing your body to use more energy and work harder.

Eating can affect your mood, too. Have you ever noticed that you can hardly move after eating a big meal? This is especially common around holidays. Faced with the special foods they have been looking forward to all year, people gobble down their meals instead of slowly enjoying what they eat. Then they shuffle over to the couch for a nap. Fatigue occurs because the body cannot concentrate on so many things at once; all of its energy is directed at digesting food. If you eat smaller portions and take plenty of time to chew your food, you won't feel so tired and full after a meal.

Sometimes even after you have eaten a large portion of food, you may still feel hungry. This happens because your body needs time to digest food completely—about twenty minutes. If you eat slowly, you will usually be full by the end of a meal. If you are a fast eater, wait about twenty minutes after you are done eating to see if you are still hungry.

Often after eating a large meal (or any meal for that matter), people crave something sweet. Instead of reaching for a candy bar, try something that is naturally sweet instead. There are many delicious choices: Fruit, such as oranges and apples, has enough natural sugar to satisfy almost any sweet tooth. A shiny red apple may not sound as exciting as a piece of chocolate cake, but it will probably satisfy your craving. Another way to deal with those pesky cravings is to brush your teeth with peppermint toothpaste after eating. This will neutralize, or balance, your taste buds, and you may find that your craving disappears after brushing.

If you do not want to go the toothpaste route and you still want your sugary snack, it is best to eat it at the end of a meal. This way, since you should already be full and satisfied, you will be likely to eat less of the sweet stuff. Too many sugary snacks can cause mood swings, high blood pressure, cavities and tooth decay, and even heart disease later in life.

Too Much Caffeine

If you are like most teens, you are probably always on the go—studying for tests, hanging out with your friends, getting involved in social activities, and attending to family responsibilities. Many teenagers do not get enough sleep. Without proper rest, it is hard to stay active throughout the day. Though every individual is different, eight to ten hours of sleep every night is ideal

Caffeine can be found in coffee, tea, soda, and chocolate.

for most teenagers. On the other hand, too much sleep can make you feel tired and sluggish. And irregular sleeping patterns can make it harder for you to think clearly or make important decisions.

Many people drink caffeinated beverages in the morning to help them wake up, and some people rely on caffeine to get them through the rest of the day. This is a bad habit. A small amount of caffeine will not cause you much harm, but it is not a good idea to depend on it to stay awake. Caffeine can be found in beverages like coffee, tea, and soft drinks. It can also be found in chocolate and over-the-counter pain medications. Too much caffeine can cause a person to become irritable, anxious, and nervous. It can cause headaches and stomach pain as well.

If you are looking for a healthier energy boost during the day, forget the caffeine and try an exercise program. A few minutes of simple stretching in the morning can help you to wake up and get your body moving. Blood flow to the muscles will give you energy and keep you awake throughout the day. If you still cannot live without caffeine, try cutting back slowly, or limit the amount you have to two small cups a day.

A lot of people like to socialize in cafes. Coffee shops are popping up all over the place. If you make the decision to cut back on caffeine, this does not mean that you can no longer hang out with your friends in these places. Most coffee shops offer plenty of alternatives to caffeinated coffee. Try ordering hot cider or herbal tea. And of course, decaffeinated coffee is always an option. Don't worry—if it's a double mocha latté that you want, that too can be made without caffeine.

The Effects of Alcohol

Alcohol is a drug that many people experiment with during their teenage years. Alcohol consumption can have long-term damaging effects on your body, especially on your liver. Also, alcohol is very high in calories and offers no nutritional value.

Drinking too much alcohol seriously affects your judgment. You may behave inappropriately or lose control of what you say. Many people who drink get themselves into very embarrassing situations, such as swearing at a girlfriend's mother or telling a friend that you have never really liked her. Alcohol use can also cause you to make bad decisions—and one of the worst decisions that you can make is to drink and drive.

Alcohol is not digested like ordinary beverages. The faster you drink an alcoholic beverage, the faster it will reach your brain and affect your thinking. This is because the alcohol doesn't have enough time to be completely absorbed by your liver. If you drink a small amount of alcohol slowly, it can be processed without much of an effect on the rest of your body.

Drinking on an empty stomach is an extremely bad thing to do. When there is no food in your system to help absorb alcohol, your senses will quickly become impaired, or unable to function properly. Alcohol also causes dehydration (the loss of liquids in the body) and the loss of certain important minerals. As you can clearly see, avoiding alcohol completely is a smart choice.

Other Beverages

It is important to pay attention not only to what you eat but also to what you are drinking. Soda and sweetened fruit juices often contain a lot of sugar. Instead try drinking 100 percent natural fruit juices like apple, orange, and pineapple. You can find out the ingredients in bottled drinks by looking at the labels. Natural fruit juices do not contain glucose or fructose, which are just fancy words for added sugar.

Water is also a very important part of a balanced diet. The Food and Drug Administration (FDA), a government-run organization that sets nutritional standards, recommends drinking eight glasses of water per day. Drinking lots of water is the best way to cleanse your body from the inside out. Water can improve your complexion and make your skin feel extraclean and soft. Don't worry about buying expensive bottled water; most tap water is just as good.

The food you put into your body affects you throughout the day. It can give you the energy you need to accomplish anything, or it can make the easiest task seem difficult. The way you treat your body is very important. If you eat food that is good for you, your mind will be clearer, and you will be able to make better decisions.

Chapter Two

The Healthy Lifestyle

*J*ames and his friends went to a fast-food restaurant every day after school. It became a tradition to meet by the lockers and head across the street for some tasty cheeseburgers. Fast food was an ideal choice for many reasons. The restaurant was close by and fairly inexpensive. But James was getting tired of going there every day, and he never felt good after eating all of those greasy fries. Even though he was sick of doing the same thing all of the time, this was the only chance James got to hang out with his pals.

James decided to continue eating with his friends. Instead of ordering the usual two cheeseburgers and fries, he started ordering a grilled chicken sandwich, a side salad, and water. James

Eating with friends is a popular social activity.

was happy with his decision. He still got to spend time with his friends, and he was able to eat a meal that wouldn't make him feel sick. Maybe he would even be able to convince them to eat somewhere healthier occasionally.

Eating well is not always easy when you have a busy life. It is easier to grab a snack from a fast-food restaurant than it is to pack a healthy lunch from home. For teenagers especially, food has always been a part of the social scene. It's difficult to be concerned with your food choices when the people around you do not seem to be the least bit worried about what they are eating.

Teenagers need a lot of food, especially during

growth spurts. You do not have to limit yourself to three meals a day. As a matter of fact, it's a good idea to have a snack every few hours. This will keep your energy levels at peak performance throughout the day. The food you eat at breakfast may not be enough to last until lunchtime. You may want to eat five small meals a day rather than three large ones. Once you learn how to choose healthy snacks, you can eat as much food as you want, whenever you want. Keep in mind that there is no such thing as "bad" foods—just bad diets.

Remember, the foods that we eat are made up of proteins, carbohydrates, fats, fiber, and various nutrients. Most foods contain a variety of vitamins and minerals that are needed to develop and maintain a healthy body, so there are many foods for you to choose from. If you eat properly and in moderation, you should receive all the vitamins and minerals your body needs.

It is a good idea to limit the amount of processed food that you eat. Processed food is treated with many additives, such as salt, preservatives, food coloring, artificial flavors, and sugar. However, just because everyone is passing around that bag of corn chips doesn't mean that you can't have a few. Again, moderation is key.

In the past few years, many fast-food restaurants have made an effort to keep up with society's growing concern with eating well by expanding their menus and offering more healthy choices. If your usual hangout does not offer anything that you find appealing, suggest trying a

Pizza, plain or with vegetables, is both tasty and healthy.

new place. If there are no other places in the area, order a salad. If you simply must have that burger, compensate by having a baked potato instead of high-fat french fries. Try ordering orange juice or water instead of soda. The decision to eat smart doesn't have to affect the time you spend hanging out with your friends.

A lot of people think that pizza is bad for you. You will be happy to know that this is actually a myth. If you like pizza, feel free to indulge—just leave off the sausage and pepperoni. The cheese on pizza has protein, the crust provides your body with carbohydrates, and the sauce is made from tomatoes, which are filled with vitamins. Remember not to get too carried away, though; you shouldn't live on pizza or eat ten slices at a time!

Fruit, vegetables, and whole-grain crackers are healthy snacks.

If your friends are planning a big party, or if football practice is next week and you've been asked to supply some snacks, you should know that there are many alternatives to chips and cheese puffs. Some healthy items that you might want to try are minibagels, crackers, sliced fruit, cut vegetables, granola bars, string cheese, popcorn, frozen yogurt, vegetable chips, and fruit juice.

Advertisements and Food

Paula and Bill were watching television when they saw a commercial for mint chocolate chip ice cream. All these beautiful people were eating ice cream, having fun, laughing, and joking around with one another. The images of ice cream made

Paula's mouth water. The thought of those extra toppings—like walnuts, sprinkles, and cherries— seemed irresistible.

Suddenly Paula was hungry. Bill reminded her that they had just eaten dinner, but he also agreed that the ice cream in the commercial looked really good. It didn't take much for Paula to convince Bill to go out and get a sundae with her. Paula ordered cookies and cream with extra sprinkles, and Bill decided on the double-fudge superchunky chocolate.

Advertising plays an important role in sending us messages about the kind of foods we eat. Television commercials, magazine ads, and billboards tempt our taste buds. Supermarkets carefully arrange their products in order to entice you to buy, buy, buy. They shelve certain foods at eye level in order to catch your attention.

Have you ever wondered why all the candy bars are near the register? While waiting in a huge line with all of your groceries, you spot that chocolate almond bar—so you grab it and throw it in with the rest of your stuff. You're already at the register, so you don't have much time to change your mind. This is called impulse buying. Advertisers and shopkeepers set up their stores this way on purpose to get you to buy these items. Would you have bought that chocolate bar if it had not been right in front of you? Would you

You are more likely to buy junk food if you don't plan ahead.

ever get out of line and go to the back of the store just to get one? Probably not. If you make the effort to plan your snacks ahead of time, you are more likely to choose something that is good for you.

Money, Money, Money

Money is often an issue that teenagers worry about when it comes to buying healthy food. Sometimes it seems as if healthy food is much more expensive and takes much more time to prepare than other foods. This is not always true. It may seem as though there aren't many places where you can find an inexpensive, well-balanced meal. You have to be creative. Ask yourself what you can do to make your meal healthier.

Check out different cookbooks for healthy meal ideas.

One alternative is to eat at home more often. Meals prepared at home can be better for you because they do not contain extra additives. You can also save money if you decide to eat something that is already in your refrigerator. If you're hungry during the day and you haven't brought any food from home, pick up a piece of fruit instead of a muffin or doughnut. Try frozen yogurt or sorbet instead of ice cream. Rather than reaching for a bag of chips, go for pretzels or crackers. All of these alternatives are about the same price as the other choices.

Whenever possible, try to bring food from home. You may think that it is impossible to make something tasty and convenient, and you may not want to spend a lot of time cooking. There are plenty of cookbooks in the library and at bookstores that cater to teenagers. If you are having a hard time finding a good cookbook, ask a librarian or bookstore employee to help you locate what you need. Let your parents know that you are interested in eating smart, and suggest that you go along with them to the grocery store to pick up some healthy items. They may even offer to help you with food preparation.

Pack a Lunch

If possible, bring your lunch to school at least three times a week. There are plenty of things you can pack. Peanut butter and jelly is everybody's favorite standby. Try sliced turkey or fresh vegetables with hummus. Throw in a piece of fruit, some unbuttered popcorn, and a boxed juice, and you have a complete, well-balanced meal. For a snack, try packing some baby carrots and sliced peppers instead of potato chips. Bring yogurt or low-fat sour cream dip in a small container and put the vegetables in a plastic bag. This way you can get the great taste of the dip, whereas the vegetables provide you with important vitamins and minerals.

Snacking

If you like to nibble on tasty snacks while doing home-work, there are plenty of healthy finger foods. Try grapes instead of M&M's. Apples with a small amount

Pack yourself a healthy
lunch several times a week.

of honey can satisfy a sweet tooth. Anything dipped in peanut butter is not only fun to eat but good for you; try celery sticks, carrots, apples, and even pretzels. Keep some trail mix with you to snack on between classes. Trail mix can be found in most health food stores, or make your own with raisins, peanuts, sunflower seeds, sesame sticks, and dried fruit. And who said that cereal is just for breakfast? Be careful, though—some cereals are loaded with sugar and don't offer many health benefits. Your best choices are whole-grain, unsweetened brands.

If you think that salad is boring, try sprucing it up with new things. See how many different vegetables you can add to one salad. Use shredded cheese and walnuts, and throw in some fruit, too. Sliced plums and tangerines taste great with cucumbers and cherry tomatoes. Experiment with different kinds of lettuce, such as arugula or romaine. Instead of a heavy salad dressing, try olive oil and vinegar, with lots of chopped garlic and fresh basil. Fruits and vegetables have incredible nutritional value, and if you eat a large portion at dinner, you're less likely to go for seconds on those buttery mashed potatoes.

Food Myths

There are many different myths about food. One of the most popular says that if you eat chocolate, your

Peanut butter is a delicious source of protein.

face will break out in pimples. There is no evidence to support this. It is true that if your diet is unhealthy, you will probably have a poor complexion. Unless you are allergic to a specific food, however, you will most likely not break out from eating it.

Another popular myth is that eating spinach will make you strong. Spinach is certainly healthy and highly nutritious, but don't rely on it to build your biceps. Eating a lot of carrots will not dramatically improve your eyesight, and an apple a day doesn't necessarily keep the doctor away either.

A lot of people think that honey is a great substitute for sugar, but in reality it has just as many calories. The same goes for brown sugar. Molasses is a slightly better alternative but is still high in sugar. Dried fruit is not as healthy as fresh fruit, but it is a better option than candy.

Do not be fooled by food labels that say "low-fat" or "nonfat." It's true that these types of foods may be low in fat, but the calorie content is often the same as the real deal. There may also be added sugar and other artificial flavorings to spruce up the taste. It is better to eat regular food in moderation rather than fat-free alternatives.

Protein drinks and energy bars are gaining in popularity, especially among athletes. These items may give you an energy boost, but they are usually high in calories and sometimes contain artificial sweeteners. It is better to get your protein by eating a balanced diet.

Everyone Is Different

Do not be concerned if your eating habits are very different from the eating habits of others. It is important to remember that every person is different. Everyone grows at a different rate and has a different body. The amount of food that your little brother eats probably would not be enough to get you through the day. Your best friend may be bigger and more active than you and therefore may eat more. You may have a more active lifestyle than your older sister, and that is why you eat more than she does. Every person's body has individual requirements for growing. So do not be alarmed if after you and your best friend share a huge salad, you are still hungry but your friend is full.

Teenagers sometimes feel that because they are young and full of energy, they are invincible. They may believe that a healthy diet is something that only older people need to worry about. But the sooner you develop healthy eating habits, the better off you will be for the rest of your life. It is helpful to think of healthy eating as a positive way of life instead of a tiresome chore. Eating smart gets easier once it becomes a habit. Remember, even when you are busy editing your high school paper or hanging out at the mall with your friends, you can still find the time to eat right.

Chapter Three

Food Pyramids for Growing Bodies

*O*lga had a very active lifestyle. She was on the track team at school and had a part-time job. She was a finicky eater; she ate only grape jelly sandwiches and an occasional tuna salad. She never felt satisfied after a meal. Olga's mother told her that she did not eat properly and that the reason she was always hungry was that she was not getting enough of the right nutrients to help her grow.

After an annual checkup with her doctor, Olga realized that she would have to change her eating habits if she wanted to stay healthy. Her doctor told her about the variety of foods she should eat to get all of the nutrition her body needed. If she didn't start eating properly, she was in danger of becoming anemic because she was not getting

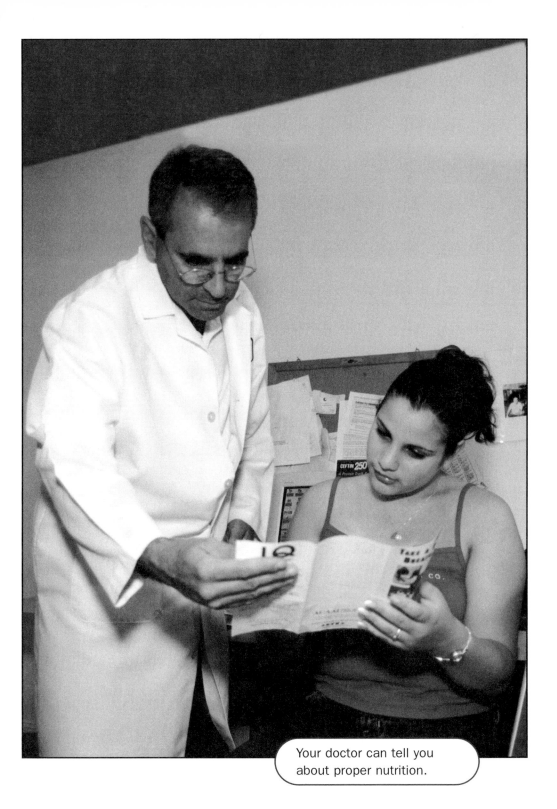

Your doctor can tell you about proper nutrition.

enough iron. She also needed more calcium in her diet. Betty asked her doctor if she could just take some vitamins. He told her that vitamins were not meant to replace food. Instead he gave her a few pamphlets to study and a chart of the food pyramid. Betty told her mother that she was going to make the extra effort to eat well.

The amount of food you need will change throughout your life. Appropriate food intake is based on your size, age, metabolism (the rate at which your body digests food), level of activity, and whether you are male or female. The FDA has created a food pyramid to help people understand what type of foods are necessary for a balanced diet. The food pyramid, made up of five basic food groups, comes with recommended servings for each group. The food groups are breads and grains, fruits and vegetables, dairy products, meat and protein products, and fats, oils, and sweets.

Breads and Grains

At the bottom of the pyramid is the breads and grains group. The number of food servings that you need from each group gets smaller as you go up the pyramid. This means that you should have more grains than fats in your diet. The recommended number of servings of grains—such as bread, cereal, rice, and pasta—is six to eleven per day. This may sound like a lot, but keep in

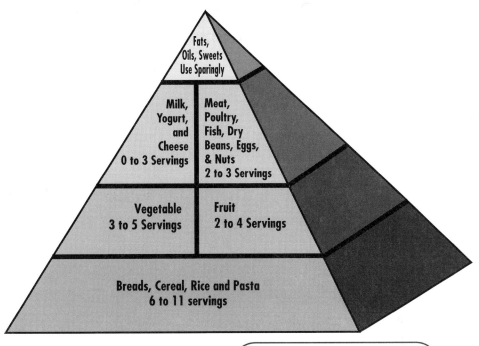

The food pyramid explains daily food serving recommendations.

mind that a serving is not a plateful. One serving is equal to one slice of bread, an ounce of cereal, or half a cup of cooked pasta.

Grains are an important part of your diet because they provide you with complex carbohydrates, which are a good source of energy. Much of the fiber your body needs comes from this food group. Although fiber does not get absorbed into the body, it aids in digestion. Fiber helps food pass through your body easily. People who eat enough fiber have less risk of obesity and of developing heart disease and certain types of cancer later in life.

Fruits and Vegetables

Fruits and vegetables are also good sources of fiber. This brings us to the second most important food group. The food pyramid recommends three to five servings of vegetables a day. One serving can include three-quarters of a cup of vegetable juice, half a cup of chopped vegetables, or a cup of leafy greens. Many vegetables are high in vitamin A and vitamin C, and all are low in fat. Two to three servings of fruit should also be eaten each day. Fresh fruit is best, but fruit juice as well as frozen, dried, and canned fruit all count. It is best to avoid fruit that has been artificially sweetened or that comes packed in heavy syrup. One apple, banana, or orange; one melon slice; a half cup of berries; or three-quarters of a cup of fruit juice all count as one serving.

Dairy Products

Dairy products, including milk products, yogurt, and cheese, should make up two to four servings of your diet each day. Dairy products are important for growing bodies because they provide a rich source of calcium, which makes your bones stronger and helps you grow. The calcium absorbed by your bones during your teenage years stays in your body for the rest of your life. If you do not get enough calcium now, your bones will become weaker and more likely to break or fracture. Women who don't get enough calcium early in life can develop a disease called osteoporosis. When osteoporosis occurs, the length and size of bones become smaller, and the bones are no longer strong

Protein can be found in nuts, legumes, tofu, and eggs.

enough to support a person's weight. Calcium can be found in eggs, cheese, tofu, milk, and even in dark leafy greens.

Meat and Protein Products

The next group is meat and protein products. This group includes meat and poultry, fish, dry beans, eggs, and nuts. Peanut butter and tofu are also part of this group. Two to three servings a day are recommended. These foods provide an excellent source of protein, iron, zinc, and vitamin B. Two to three ounces of cooked meat, one egg, or a half cup of beans are all considered one serving.

Iron is important at any age. If you are not getting enough iron in your diet, you may feel tired and weak and be more likely to develop infections. As a general rule, females need more iron than males because they lose iron when they menstruate. Athletes also require more iron because they lose a lot of it when they sweat. Luckily iron can be found in most of the food groups.

If you eat a vegetarian diet, you can still get all the nutrition you need from meat substitutes, including tofu, tempeh, and seitan, and beans, such as chick peas. Foods from the meat and dairy groups should be eaten in moderation, meaning that you should have less from these groups than from the breads and grains group and the fruits and vegetables group.

Fats, Oils, and Sweets

Fats, oils, and sweets make up the fifth and smallest group of the pyramid. These foods should be eaten in very limited amounts in your diet. However, do not avoid fats altogether. In moderation they are an important part of your food intake and contribute to your overall health. Foods from this group also make eating a lot more enjoyable because fats help us to feel full and satisfied.

A Basic Guide to Healthy Eating

The food pyramid should be used as a basic guide for all the nutrients needed for a balanced diet. Don't worry—you do not need to follow the guide so strictly that you are constantly worrying about whether or not you have eaten the right amount of servings from each group. Remember, it is only a guide. Eating a variety of foods is important so that you can get all of the different vitamins and minerals that you need. Eating only one type of food, even if it's a healthy one, is not sufficient. Even if you like carrot and cream cheese sandwiches so much that you could eat them every day for a year, this is not a good idea. Also, one food group should not be replaced by or substituted for another; be sure to select foods from each group.

Most teenagers need at least fifty grams of protein per day. Protein can be found in many foods. It's a myth that you can get it only by eating meat. However, most people get much more protein than their bodies actually need. Protein is important for growth and energy, but you cannot build muscles simply by eating a lot of protein-rich foods. The only way to increase the size of your muscles is through exercise.

Teenagers who are not getting the nutrients they need from food often rely on vitamins. Vitamins are a fine supplement to your diet, but by no means should they be used to replace actual food. There are thirteen known vitamins that are important to human development. If your body does not get these vitamins, it will show signs of deficiency, meaning that the way you look or feel will be altered because your body is not receiving what it needs to work properly. Although it is healthier to get vitamins and minerals directly from food rather than by taking pills, vitamins are not bad for you, in appropriate amounts. It is best to discuss the benefits and shortcomings of vitamins with your doctor or another trained health care professional.

Chapter Four

Body Basics

Test taking, relationship problems, and family issues are just a few things that can cause stress. Some people react to stress by turning to food for comfort. Others avoid food altogether. It is not healthy to let stress influence or control your eating habits.

Even positive things in your life—such as a new job, a vacation, or the start of a romantic relationship—can cause stress. Eating smart means giving your mind and body what they need to work effectively. Unfortunately, during stressful times people often stop paying attention to food. They end up skipping meals or grabbing a bag of potato chips for lunch. Many things can be done to avoid falling into such traps. If you find yourself craving a certain food, try to figure out why. Do you feel a need for sugar or caffeine because you did not get enough sleep? Have you been studying for tests all week and just haven't had time for meals?

Why People Eat Certain Foods

It is important to be aware of why you choose to eat certain foods. Think about why you eat. Are you eating for reasons other than hunger? Do you do other things while eating, like watching television or talking on the phone? Try to eat before you become so hungry that you stuff yourself. If you wait until you're starving, you are much more likely to make unwise food choices.

Some people eat because they are bored. This is a bad habit, but once you recognize it, it is easy to break. If you are craving a snack, try not to eat a whole bag of corn chips. Instead, put some chips in a bowl so that you will know how much you are eating. If you want a more healthy finger food, try popping your own popcorn. It's fun, easy, and cheap, and you can control the amount of salt and butter you use.

Sometimes people eat when they are upset or nervous. Food will not make your worries go away. Instead, when you are upset, try talking about your feelings with someone you trust. Participate in an activity that makes you feel good about yourself. People also have a tendency to reward themselves with food. If you have finally aced a math test, it's definitely cause for celebration—but instead of gobbling down a whole carton of ice cream, buy yourself a new CD.

Try to limit your snacking when talking on the phone.

Alternative Diets

Ted grew up in a family that ate meat for dinner every night. During his freshman year of high school, Ted began to date Clara. Clara was a vegetarian. She would not eat meat because she believed that it was morally wrong to kill animals. She also knew that a vegetarian diet offered many health benefits. Ted didn't know a lot about vegetarianism, but he liked Clara. The problem was that he wanted Clara to enjoy the same foods that he did. He thought that her reasons for not eating meat were silly. Clara liked Ted, but she wanted him to respect her beliefs.

One night Clara invited Ted over for dinner. She served hot dogs and a big Greek salad. Ted commented on the delicious taste of the hot dogs. When Clara told him that they were made from soy and not meat, Ted laughed. After that, he decided to make an effort to be more open minded. Eventually he found himself enjoying other meat-free dishes.

As a teenager, you are able to make many of your own decisions. You are developing your own ideas and opinions about the world around you. Until now, you have probably eaten mostly what was served to you at home. But many teenagers move toward alternative diets, and more and more young adults are

A vegetarian diet can be both healthy and delicious.

choosing vegetarianism. Vegetarians are people who choose not to eat meat for health reasons, moral reasons, or because of taste preferences.

There are several different kinds of vegetarians. People who are partial vegetarians eat dairy products, eggs, fish, and possibly poultry, but not red meat. Lacto-vegetarians do not eat meat, chicken, or fish, but they do eat dairy products. Ovo-vegetarians eat eggs but don't eat meat or dairy products. Vegans do not eat any products that come from an animal.

Because of the growing popularity of vegetarianism, a meatless food pyramid has been developed. The vegetarian pyramid is similar to the traditional pyramid discussed in chapter three. The only difference is that the meat group is replaced by legumes, nuts,

More food options are available to vegetarians than ever before.

seeds, and meat alternatives. Meat alternatives—including vegetarian burgers and hot dogs, tempeh, seitan, and tofu—are generally low in fat and high in protein. These products can be found in many supermarkets and health food stores. Many restaurants that are not strictly vegetarian now cater to people who want to eat a healthy diet. A lot of menus offer at least a few vegetarian choices.

If you choose a vegetarian diet, you may have to plan your meals a little bit more carefully in order to get all of the right nutrients. Most meats provide complete proteins, meaning that they give you the essential amino acids your body needs. It is important for vegetarians to eat the right combinations of foods in order to get complete proteins. Fortunately this is easy. To get complete proteins in your diet, you can combine corn or rice with beans, lentils, or peas. You can also pair wheat with soy products, or legumes with nuts and seeds. Combining dairy products such as milk, cheese, or yogurt with potatoes, brown rice, or beans is another great way to get protein.

Vegetarians don't need to take vitamins unless they choose a vegan diet. As vegetarians age, their cholesterol level usually remains low, and they are less likely to develop heart disease. But just because you do not eat meat doesn't mean that it is okay to eat greasy french fries and chocolate bars every day. You still have to make an effort to choose healthy foods and eat smart.

Chapter Five

Dieting and Eating Disorders

Our society is obsessed with size and weight. Turn on the television or flip through a magazine, and everyone you see is thin and beautiful. The models look as if they haven't eaten for weeks. These unreasonable standards of weight and size have a bad influence on people, especially teenagers.

The media play a big role in suggesting how we should look. Being constantly bombarded by images of thin actors and models can affect one's self-image in a negative way. When we compare ourselves to the excessively thin people on television and in the movies, we often feel dissatisfied and unhappy with how we look. This can contribute to the development of eating disorders like anorexia nervosa and bulimia nervosa.

Renée's Story

Renée weighs ninety-eight pounds and is five feet five inches tall. She thinks that she is too fat. Renée often flips through magazines and wonders if she will ever look like the models she sees on every page. Renée hardly eats, and when she does she feels guilty about it. Her free time is spent exercising. She counts the calories of everything she eats at each meal, and then she calculates how much exercise she will have to do in order to burn them off. Every time she sees a thin person on the street, she gets really jealous and decides that she has to work harder at losing weight. When people tell her that she is getting too thin, she takes it as a compliment.

Soon Renée began to have trouble concentrating in school. She was exhausted all the time. Finally her mother became concerned and took her to the family doctor, who told Renée that she had an eating disorder called anorexia nervosa. The doctor recommended that Renée start seeing a therapist to help her understand her obsession with weight and food.

Anorexia nervosa is a disorder that develops when a person loses weight by starving himself or herself. A person is considered anorexic when body weight drops to fifteen percent below normal, yet this person

People with eating disorders should seek professional help.

continues to think that he or she is overweight. Anorexia can cause many serious problems, including malnutrition, loss of menstruation, and overall poor health. The disorder can affect how your internal organs work and can even cause vision problems. In extreme cases, anorexia can lead to death.

Bulimia nervosa is another eating disorder that affects many teenagers. A bulimic person may starve him- or herself for days and then binge, or eat an excessive amount. After bingeing, a bulimic will rid the system of the food, usually by vomiting or using laxatives. This vicious cycle is known as bingeing and purging. Bulimics typically become very good at hiding this behavior, so it is not unusual for family and friends to be unaware that someone close to them is suffering from bulimia.

Eating disorders mostly affect girls between the ages of fourteen and seventeen. Though both anorexia and bulimia are more common among women and girls, men and boys also suffer from these conditions. These disorders are prevalent in well-developed nations. In countries such as the United States, Canada, England, and France, the message that thinness equals happiness is far too common.

Self-esteem plays a very important role in eating disorders. When people feel good about themselves, they will not want to do things that are self-destructive. Remember, what is a normal weight for one person is not necessarily the same for another. A person's ideal weight depends on genetics, height, age, exercise level, and percentage of body fat. Muscle weighs more than fat, so someone who is lean and muscular might weigh more than someone who has more body fat.

Quick-Fix Diets

Eating smart does not deprive you of food or leave you feeling hungry. Diet fads, such as the cabbage diet, the grapefruit diet, and liquid diets, promise quick weight loss. Many of these diets work for a brief time, but as soon as the dieter returns to regular eating habits, all of the lost weight is gained back. People who follow these quick-fix diets usually see their weight go up and down. This is called yo-yo dieting, and it is not a healthy way to live. These diets can be dangerous because they do not supply you with all the nutrients you need to be healthy.

Another type of diet that is unhealthy is one frequently used by teenage boys who participate in wrestling. Coaches tell their athletes to stop eating for a few days before a competition or to eat only a certain type of food. This is done so that the boys can train in one weight category but compete in a lighter one.

Many teenagers also rely on nutritional drinks and bars. Pills, powders, liquids, and other food substitutes should not be used in place of real food. It is important to enjoy your meals. Part of feeling satisfied includes sitting down and actually chewing your food—enjoying not only the taste but the smell and the texture too.

Being Overweight

Although it is dangerous to be too thin, it can also be unhealthy to be overweight. There are many causes for obesity, including a lack of exercise, poor diet, and genetics. Some overweight people don't actually eat that much food, but if they are inactive, they will burn less energy. For some people, obesity is a problem that runs in their families, passed down from one generation to the next. This does not necessarily

Diet shakes are a poor substitute for real food.

It is important for everyone to eat well and exercise.

mean that if you have a heavy parent, you too are going to be overweight. It does mean that you have a greater chance of gaining excess weight and that you may have to be particularly careful about your diet and lifestyle.

Making a Commitment to Health

When you decide to change your eating habits, it should be a long-term commitment. Drastic changes in your diet that last only a few days will make you frustrated. Instead, set smaller goals that are easy to reach. You don't have to swear off chocolate forever. Slowly cut down on the amount of junk food that you eat. Switch from soda to seltzer or fruit juice, or drink skim or soy milk instead of whole milk.

Realize that you are a unique individual. Feel good about yourself and understand that your body weight does not define who you are. The retouched and air-brushed images of supermodels in magazines should not have the power to set the standards for everybody else. If you eat smart, you will be healthy inside and out.

Glossary

alternatives Different choices or options.

amino acid Organic acid that forms proteins necessary for all life.

anemic Condition that causes physical weakness due to a lack of iron.

anorexia nervosa Eating disorder characterized by an obsession with weight loss.

bulimia nervosa Eating disorder characterized by eating large quantities of food, followed by self-induced vomiting or laxative abuse.

calcium Mineral that helps with the growth of bones and teeth.

deficiency Lacking something that is essential.

fad diet Typically unhealthy diet that interests people for a short time and then is abandoned.

moderation Having something in a limited or controlled quantity.

neutralize To destroy or work against the effectiveness of something.

nourishment Being provided with substances necessary to live and grow.

nutrition Process by which your body gets the vitamins and minerals needed to live.

osteoporosis Bone condition characterized by a decrease in bone mass, causing bones to become brittle and break more easily.

protein Substance found in food that is essential to the human body.

supplement Something added to make up for a lack of something else.

tofu Versatile food made from soybeans; sometimes called bean curd.

vegetarian Type of diet that excludes meat.

vitamins Substances found in food that are essential to good health.

Where to Go for Help

Web Sites

KidsHealth
http://www.kidshealth.org/teen/nutrition/index.html

Nutrition Café
http://nutrition.central.vt.edu

Nutrition on the Web for Teens
http://library.advanced.org/10991

Ten Tips to Eating Healthy and Physical Activity
http://ificinfo.health.org/brochure/10tipkid.htm

You Are What You Eat: A Guide to Good Nutrition
http://library.advanced.org/11163/gather/
    cgi-bin/wookie.cgi

For Further Reading

Carpenter, Dana and Woody Winfree, eds. *I Am Beautiful: A Celebration of Women in Their Own Words.* Bridgeport, CT: Rose Communications, 1996.

Isler, Charlotte and David Kelley. *The Watts Teen Health Dictionary.* Danbury, CT: Franklin Watts, 1996.

Kane, June Kozak. *Coping With Diet Fads.* New York: Rosen Publishing Group, 1990.

Kubersky, Rachel. *Eating Disorders.* New York: Rosen Publishing Group, 1998.

Lynch, Chris. *Slot Machine.* New York: HarperCollins, 1995.

Price, Deirdra. *The Diet-Free Solution to Lifelong Weight Management:* New York: Plume, 1998.

Salter, Charles. *The Nutrition-Fitness Link.* Brookfield, CT: Millbrook Press, 1993.

Salter, Charles. *The Vegetarian Teen.* Brookfield, CT: Millbrook Press, 1991.

Sommers, Annie Leah. *Everything You Need to Know About Looking and Feeling Your Best: A Guide for Girls.* New York: Rosen Publishing Group, 1999.

Sommers, Michael A. *Everything You Need to Know About Looking and Feeling Your Best: A Guide for Guys.* New York: Rosen Publishing Group, 1999.

Index

Index

About the Author

Aileen Weintraub is an editor and writer residing in Brooklyn, New York. She is the author of *Everything You Need to Know About Baby-sitting* and is currently working on a series of children's books. Aileen enjoys creating new recipes and whipping up healthy cuisine to suit her vegetarian lifestyle.

Photo Credits

Cover by Shalhevet Moshe. P. 47 by Thaddeus Harden; all other photos by Shalhevet Moshe.

Design and Layout

Annie O'Donnell